Easy-to-Make Appliqué Quilts for Children

Instructions & Full-Size Templates

Judith Hoffman Corwin

Dover Publications, Inc., New York

Copyright © 1982 by Dover Publications, Inc.
All rights reserved under Pan American and International Copyright Conventions.

Published in Canada by General Publishing Company, Ltd., 30 Lesmill Road, Don Mills, Toronto, Ontario.
Published in the United Kingdom by Constable and Company, Ltd., 10 Orange Street, London WC2H 7EG.

Easy-to-Make Appliqué Quilts for Children is a new work, first published by Dover Publications, Inc., in 1982.

Edited by Linda Macho
Book design by Paula Goldstein

Manufactured in the United States of America
Dover Publications, Inc.
180 Varick Street
New York, N.Y. 10014

Library of Congress Cataloging in Publication Data

Corwin, Judith Hoffman.
    Easy-to-make appliqué quilts for children.
    1. Quilting. 2. Appliqué. I. Title.
TT835.C67   746.9′7   81-17331
ISBN 0-486-24293-5 (pbk.)   AACR2

Contents

INTRODUCTION	5
METRIC CONVERSION CHART	10
Cat	11
Owl	11
Elephant	12
Butterfly	12
House	13
Duck	13
Turtle	14
Teddy Bear	14
Heart	15
Bunny	15
Ladybug	16
Ball	16
TEMPLATE SECTION	Plates A-P

Introduction

Appliqué is the process of applying one piece of fabric to another by sewing; the applied piece is usually decorative. A folk art which developed from the craft of pieced patchwork, appliqué lends itself to geometric forms and natural shapes such as flowers, butterflies, birds, and other animals. During the 1800's, appliqué as a quilt form reached its height in America; the choice quilts of the day were appliquéd with elaborate floral designs that were a showcase for the creator's needlework skill and imagination. The beautiful quilts that came out of this era were frequently given as wedding gifts or were made to commemorate some other special event in a family's life.

Almost anything that can be drawn can be put onto cloth through appliqué. The required supplies, tools, and materials are inexpensive and readily available, and the only skill requirement is an ability to cut, press, and stitch. Anyone can appliqué—from a child to the most experienced needleworker. Appliqué can be as simple or as fanciful and complicated as the stitcher wishes. A heart shape stitched over a worn spot on a child's jeans is just as much a piece of appliqué as the finest piece of linen embellished with many small fabric pieces.

This book contains designs for twelve easy-to-make appliqué blocks. For each design, there are actual-size templates printed on heavy paper which can be used to cut out the necessary fabric pieces. Two simple embroidery stitches are recommended for the finishing details on many blocks—the satin stitch and the outline stitch; these stitches are illustrated on page 8.

Each design should be appliquéd on a 12" square. One square is large enough for a child's pillow covering, four squares will produce a small quilt suitable for a wall hanging in a child's room, six squares will make a medium-size quilt and twelve squares will create a large quilt. As you can imagine, the designs in this book have an unlimited number of creative possibilities. The twelve designs can be used in any combination to produce any number of children's quilts—for instance, you can make a teddy-bear quilt, a quilt with teddy bears and hearts, or a multiform quilt such as the one featured on the front cover of this book. In addition, you can vary the block size as well as the placement of the blocks. Also, the use of diverse colors and prints can make the same two quilts appear entirely different!

The experience of selecting different colors and arranging the designs in a way that is pleasing will be an enjoyable challenge and will result in a unique and functional piece of handiwork that will be a welcome addition to any household. Your pleasure and pride in completing each quilt block will only be enhanced by the sight of a child peacefully asleep under the quilt you have lovingly stitched.

Equipment and Supplies

To make your work more enjoyable and to ensure a beautifully finished quilt, the proper equipment is necessary. All equipment should be clean and in good condition. Your fabric scissors should not be used for any other household jobs. Pins and needles should be rust-free and perfectly straight.

Keep your equipment organized and in one place; this will enable you to pick up your work whenever you have a spare moment without wasting time searching for a piece of fabric or the proper color thread. A medium-size basket or box would be suitable for storage of equipment; appliqué pieces and templates should be stored in labeled envelopes.

Fabric

Soft, closely woven fabrics such as gingham, calico, and percale hold seams well and the fabric edges will not fray easily when cut. Fabric that is made from 100% cotton gives the best results because cotton is easy to work with and wears much better than any other type of fabric. However, a small amount of polyester combined with cotton may increase the washability of the fabric, although more than 30% synthetic-fiber content in the fabric will make it difficult to work with and reduce wearability. Do not combine used fabrics with new ones. Work with fabrics that have been pre-shrunk and those which are color-fast.

It is also a good idea to wash all fabrics in hot water before using them. Reds and dark blue fabrics tend to bleed if the original dyeing was done carelessly, and washing the fabric will also remove any sizing that might be in it. After washing, all fabrics should be freshly pressed before you begin to work. Check the grain line of the fabric carefully. Lengthwise threads should be parallel to the selvage and crosswise threads exactly perpendicular to the selvage to ensure that the pieces will be correctly cut. If the fabric seems off-grain, pull it to straighten—do this on the true bias in the direction opposite the off-grain edge. Continue stretching until the crosswise threads are at right angles to the lengthwise threads. When using a fabric with a design, choose one with a small pattern in keeping with the scale of the actual appliqué piece.

Fabric Amounts

You will need to cut 13" squares of fabric for your background blocks; this measurement includes a ½" seam allowance on all four sides. After cutting out the 13" square, any extra material can be used to make up the different appliqué pieces for the various other quilt blocks. You will also need fabric for the back (or lining) of the quilt; make sure this fabric is compatible with the fabric you are using for the quilt top. 1½ yards of 36"-wide fabric is enough for a twelve-block quilt; adjust the yardage accordingly for a smaller or larger quilt.

Needles

For appliqué work, use "Sharps," which are medium-length needles most commonly used for hand sewing. Use crewel needles for all embroidery work.

Thread

Use color-fast threads which match the appliqué fabric; any high-quality mercerized cotton or polyester thread will be suitable. Cotton thread may shrink when washed and cause unwanted puckers in the fabric, so it is advisable to use a polyester thread if the quilt is going to be laundered frequently.

Scissors

Use very sharp dressmaker shears to cut the larger appliqué pieces and quilt blocks; use good embroidery scissors for the smaller pieces and for cutting threads.

Pins

Pin all the appliqué pieces in place before they are basted; straight pins should be clean and in good condition.

Thimble

The thimble is a good sewing aid and will save wear and tear on your finger; if you find it uncomfortable to use a thimble, a piece of adhesive tape on the tip of your middle finger will protect it.

Pencils

Use sharp, soft-lead pencils for tracing around the outline of each template. If you are using dark fabrics or fabrics with a busy print, use tailor's chalk or light-colored marking pencils.

Iron

Ironing is necessary for professional results in appliqué work. Spend a little time pressing the appliqué pieces after the ¼" seam has been turned to the wrong side. Use a damp press cloth to make sharp edges.

Batting

When the quilt is ready to be assembled, batting is used in between the top and the lining to give warmth and loft to the finished quilt. Batting can be cotton or polyester. I used polyester batting because it is machine-washable, will dry quickly without lumping, and is available in large pre-cut seamless sheets. It is readily available in fabric shops and department, hobby, and craft stores or through mail order from quilt companies.

Tips for Successful Appliqué Work

Prepare each block with great care and attention to detail. All fabric edges must be smooth and unraveled. Each piece of the design must lie flat on the quilt block, with no wrinkles sewn permanently into either the appliqué or the background fabric. Sewing construction, whether by hand or machine, must be neat and strong.

<u>Using the Templates</u>

All the actual-size templates for each design are printed on heavyweight paper in the template section of this book. Refer to the color and black-and-white photographs of each quilt block, and read the specific directions for each before beginning to work. The photographs and directions will illustrate proper placement of the appliqué pieces and will give instructions for the finishing touches.

To start, cut out the required templates from the book. It is important that all templates be cut out carefully because if they are inaccurate, the appliqué pieces will not fit together correctly. Use a pair of sharp paper scissors, a single-edged razor blade or an X-acto knife to do the cutting. When necessary, trace around your original template and make a duplicate from heavy cardboard, discarding the old one as it becomes frayed; you will probably need a new set of templates for every four or five blocks. To prevent excess fraying, paint the edges of each template with several coats of clear nail polish, allowing the nail polish to harden between each coat; this will extend the life of your templates considerably.

Pin the templates in place on the wrong side of the fabric. Position each template so that as much of the contour of the shape as possible is on the bias or near-bias of the fabric; this saves fabric and ensures a smooth edge when the seam allowance is turned to the wrong side. The seam allowance requires an additional ¼" all around the edges of the template; this should be taken into account when positioning the templates on the fabric. A ½" margin between templates and raw edges or selvages will provide for the seam allowance.

Once the template is pinned in place, carefully mark around its edge with a sharp pencil. This line should be accurate and neat as it shows the outer dimensions of the finished piece; it will also be a guide for clipping the seam allowance. Sketch a cutting line ¼" away from the outline, trying to make the curves as smooth as possible.

Cutting

Cut out the appliqué pieces along the sketched cutting line (Diagram 1); you must cut carefully and accurately so that the pieces fit together perfectly. Clip into the seam allowance at right angles to the penciled line, being careful to clip just to, but not through the line (Diagram 2). Make clips at wide intervals on curves that are gradual or nearly straight and close together where curves are sharp; this allows the fabric to lie flat when stitched to the quilt block.

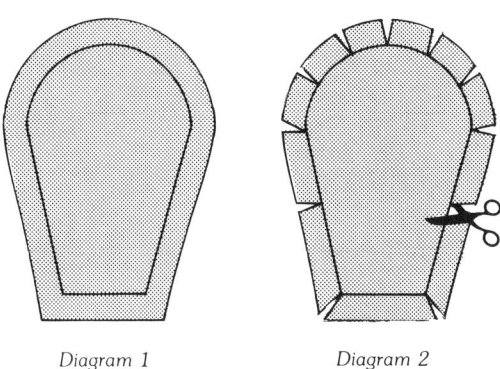

Diagram 1   *Diagram 2*

Basting

Basting is a necessary and crucial step in the process of appliqué. It requires an investment of time but when carefully done, will assure that each appliqué piece is the exact shape of the template. Choose a thread color to contrast with the appliqué fabric; this will make it easier to remove all the basting stitches when the appliqué is completed. To baste, hold the fabric piece wrong side up, folding the ¼" seam allowance to the wrong side—the pencil line on the fabric is your fold guide. Secure the fold with a series of small basting stitches (Diagram 3); take care that all clipped sections of the seam allowance are secured. Folding carefully on the marked line, proceed along the edge of the piece, making a backstitch when ending a length of thread.

After you have basted all the edges of the appliqué, the next step is to baste the piece in place onto the quilt block. All the designs for the quilt blocks are centered on the background fabric; therefore the center point of the square must be established. Measure and mark the center of each side edge of the background square. Baste a vertical center line from top to bottom; baste a horizontal center line from side to side. Basting lines will cross in the exact center of the square. Press the background square. Following the individual directions, baste the appliqué pieces in place, centered on the background (Diagram 4). Do not pin-baste the pieces because pins tend to fall out while handling the work.

Hand Appliqué

The quilt on the cover of this book was appliquéd by hand. The main objective of hand appliqué is to achieve an appearance of overall neatness—the size and uniformity of the stitches will greatly affect the look of the finished quilt. I have used the *blind* or *invisible* stitch. The benefit of using this stitch is that slight irregularities in the size and placement of the stitches will not show. Further, since the thread is not exposed to direct wear, the quilt will last a long time.

Cut a length of thread about 18" long and thread the needle, making a knot at the opposite end of the thread. Too long a length of thread will cause it to knot or become tangled. Once the needle is threaded, draw it through the quilt block from the wrong side, catching the folded edge of the appliqué piece. Following Diagram 5, guide the point of the needle into the quilt block, being sure to catch two or three threads, then back into the edge of the fold; now draw the needle up and pull the thread snugly for your first stitch. The needle is always drawn up from the right side of the appliqué—not from the back. The needle should be guided only into the fold where the seam allowance is turned under; it should not come through the top surface of the appliqué fabric. Keep in mind that small, even stitches look best and that there should be no

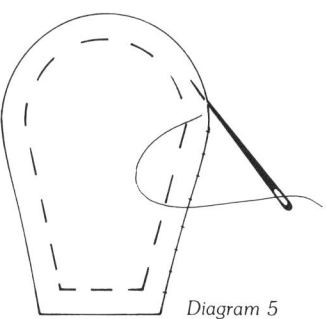

Diagram 5

wrinkles or frayed edges. Don't be discouraged if there are slight irregularities in the size and placement of your stitches since the thread should blend in with the color of the appliqué. Several overcast stitches worked close together will reinforce the appliqué wherever some unraveling has occurred or where clipping has left a tiny seam allowance. To end the thread, return the needle to the wrong side of the quilt block and either make a knot or make two or three small backstitches. Now clip the thread and begin work on the next piece to be appliquéd. After finishing all sewing, remove the basting threads and steam-press each quilt block thoroughly.

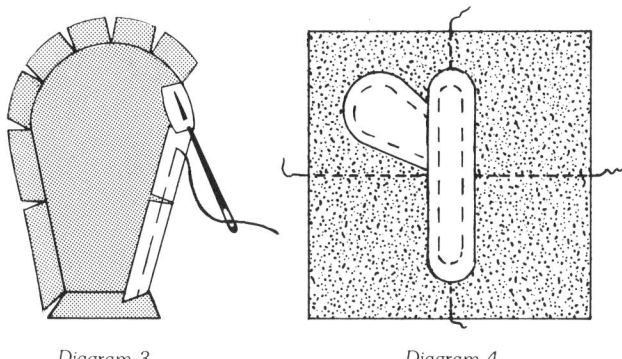

Diagram 3   *Diagram 4*

Machine Appliqué

Appliqué work can be quick and easy when stitched by machine. Mark the appliqué pieces on the appropriate fabrics, sketching in the ¼" seam allowance as directed. Cut out all pieces along the sketched cutting line, then baste to the background fabric without turning under the edges. Machine-sew the pieces to the background along the original outline, making 10–12 stitches per inch (Diagram 6), and trim away the excess seam allowance to ⅛" from the machine stitching (Diagram 7). Set your sewing machine for a close zigzag satin stitch; with matching thread, sew around the edge of each appliqué, covering the straight stitches and excess fabric (Diagram 8).

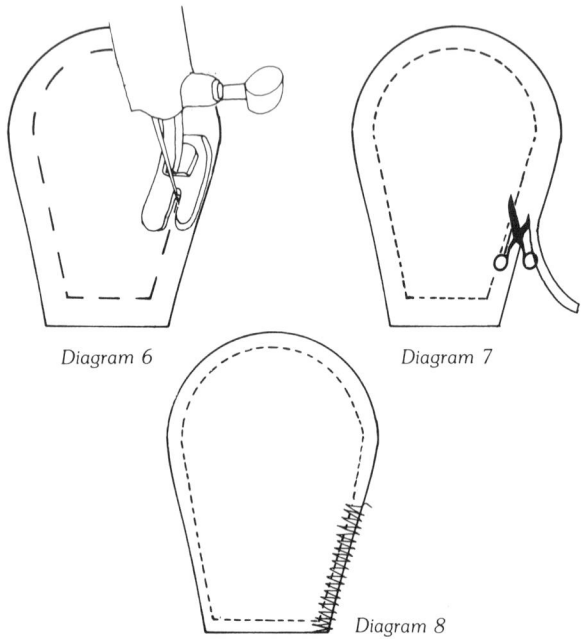

Diagram 6 *Diagram 7*

Diagram 8

Embroidered Details

Embroidery will add dimension, color and texture to your appliquéd blocks. Pearl cotton or six-strand embroidery floss should be used, in a color which contrasts with the fabric to be embroidered.

Satin stitch is used to fill a large area such as an eye or a heart; outline stitch is used to delineate a thin line such as an antenna or a mouth. First, trace the embroidery pattern. Transfer the design to the right side of the fabric to be embroidered as follows: Place the fabric right side up on a flat surface. Place a piece of dressmaker's carbon paper over the fabric, then center the pattern over the fabric and the dressmaker's carbon. Pin in place. Trace around all the design lines using a hard lead pencil or a *dry* ball-point pen. Remove the pattern and carbon. Stretch the area to be embroidered in an embroidery hoop to hold the fabric taut; embroider the design in satin or outline stitch following the individual directions and the stitch details above right.

Begin embroidering by leaving the end of the floss on the back of the fabric and stitching over it to secure; do not make knots. To end a strand or begin a new one, weave the floss under the stitching on the back. If the floss begins to kink or twist while you are working, allow the needle and floss to hang straight down to unwind.

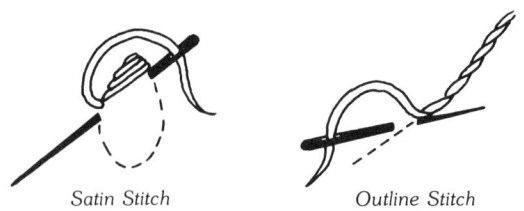

Satin Stitch *Outline Stitch*

Assembling the Quilt

A quilt consists of three parts: the top, the batting and the lining. To assemble the top, position the completed blocks on a flat surface in the shape of a quilt; the size of the quilt will vary according to the number of blocks you have made. Study your arrangement, then reposition the blocks so that colors and appliqué shapes are displayed to their best advantage. When you are satisfied with the placement of the blocks, join adjacent blocks in horizontal rows by sewing them together, right sides facing, making ½" seams. Press the seam allowances to one side, preferably toward the darker fabric. Next, join the rows of blocks in the same way, making sure the seams match perfectly (Diagram 9), sew together, then press the seam allowances to one side.

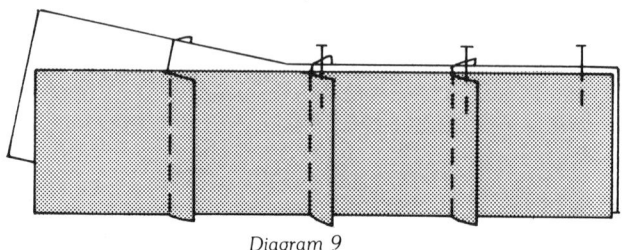

Diagram 9

After the quilt top is assembled, use it as a pattern to cut the batting and the lining. Cut a layer of batting the same size as the quilt top. The total size of the lining should allow for a 2" margin on all sides of the quilt top; the margin of lining fabric will be used to bind the quilt. If the quilt-plus-margin width is larger than the width of your lining fabric, sew two pieces of lining fabric together to make the required size; press the seam allowance to one side. Place the lining fabric on a large flat surface so it is smooth and unwrinkled; center the quilt top over the lining fabric. Using a measuring tape and pencil, mark a cutting line on the lining fabric 2" away from the edge of the quilt top; cut out along the marked line.

Arrange the lining, wrong side up, on a large flat surface. Center the layer of batting on the lining, leaving 2" margins around all edges of the batting. Position the quilt top, right side up, over the batting. Pin layers together horizontally, vertically and diagonally (Diagram 10) using large safety pins. Baste the layers together around the edges of the quilt top. Fold the

Instructions continue following template section.

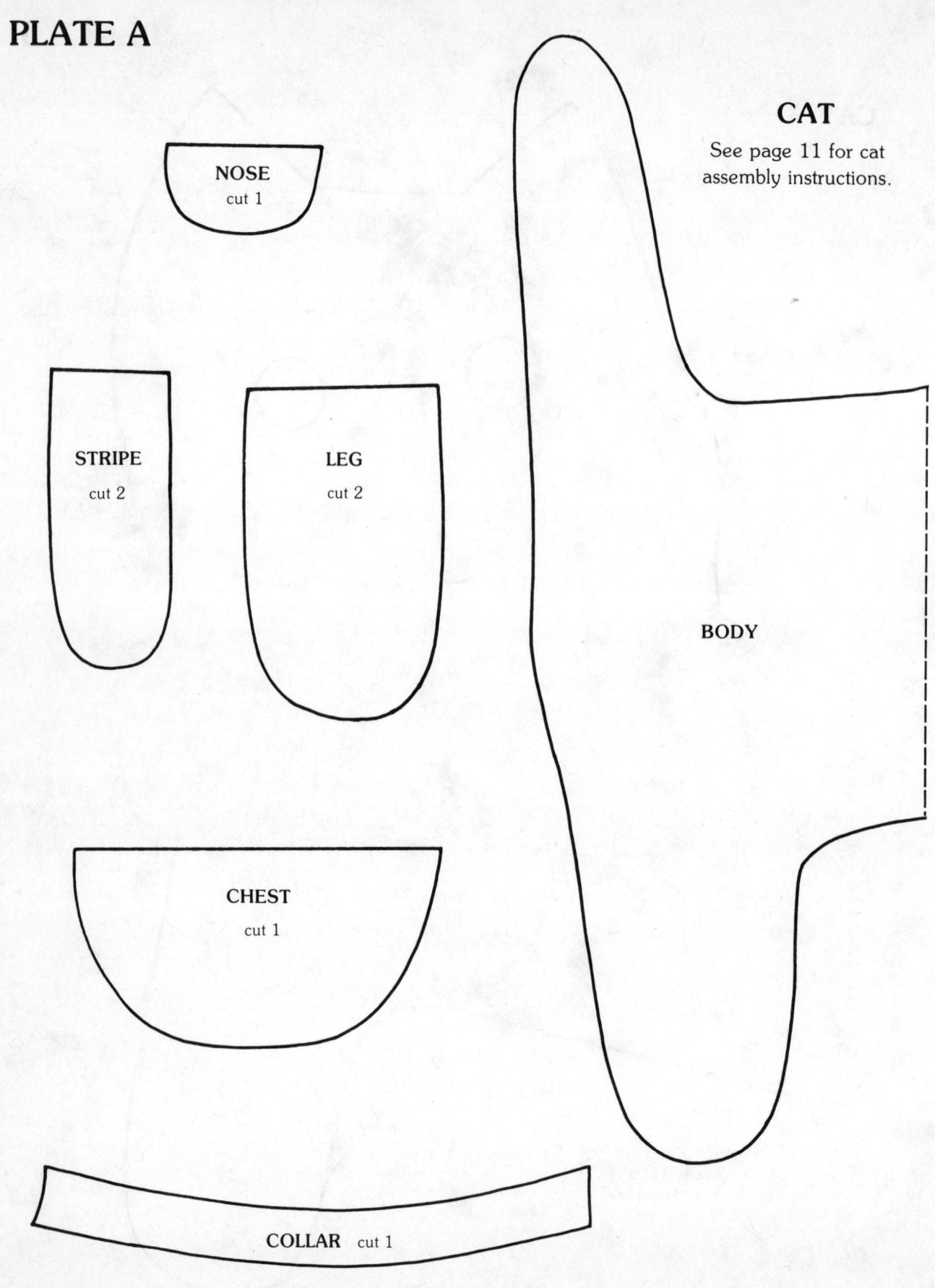

PLATE C

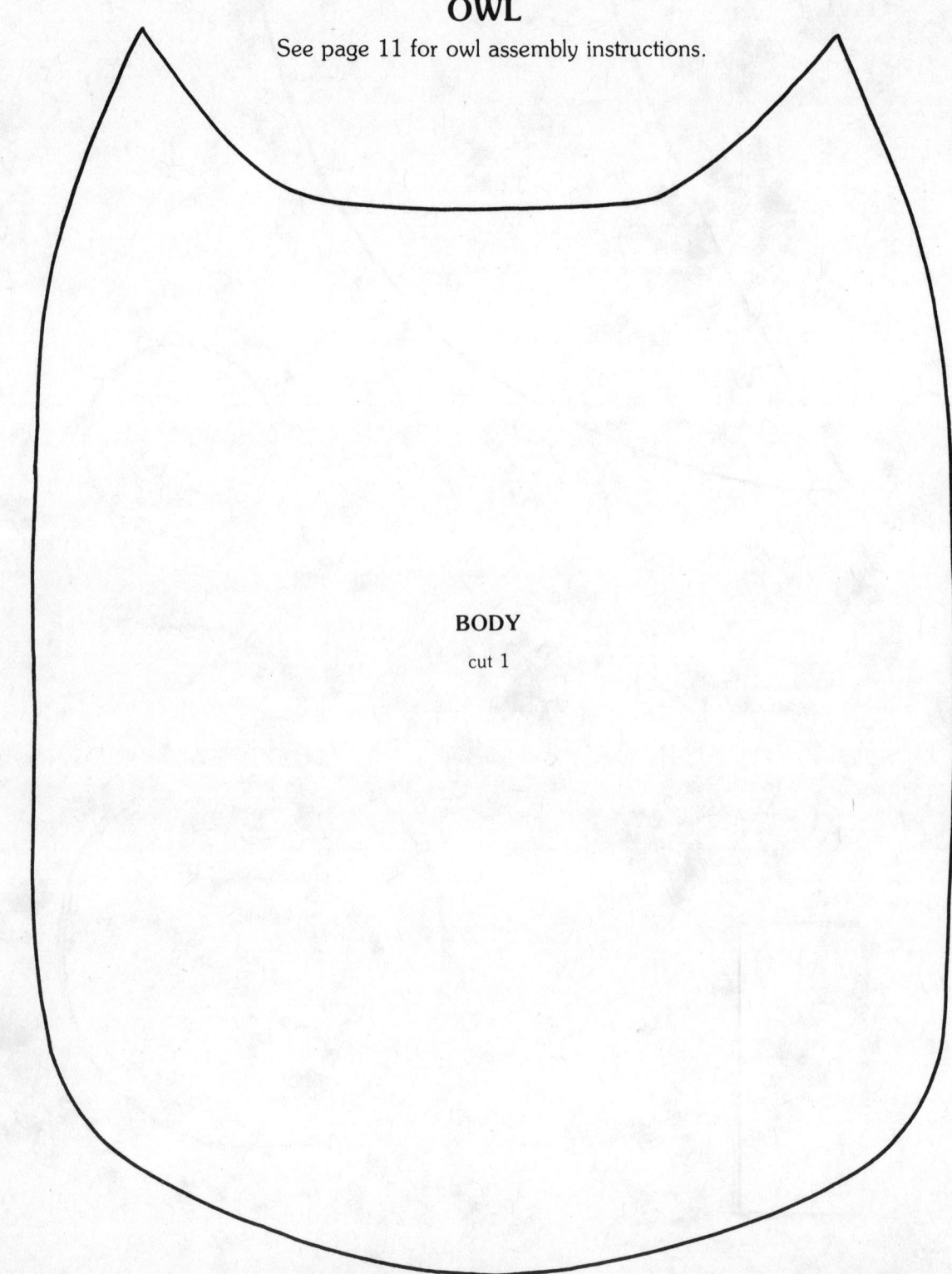

OWL
See page 11 for owl assembly instructions.

BODY
cut 1

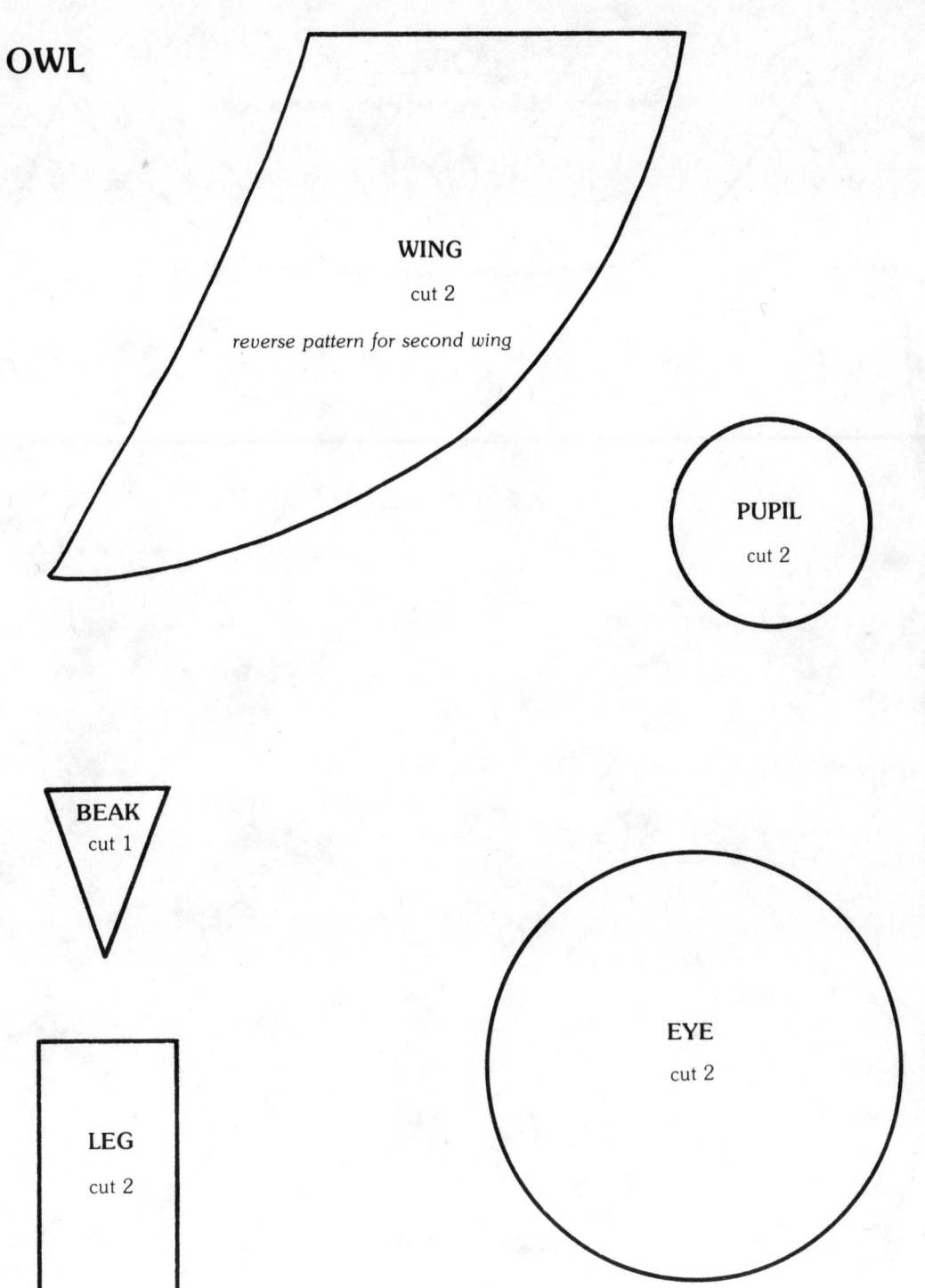

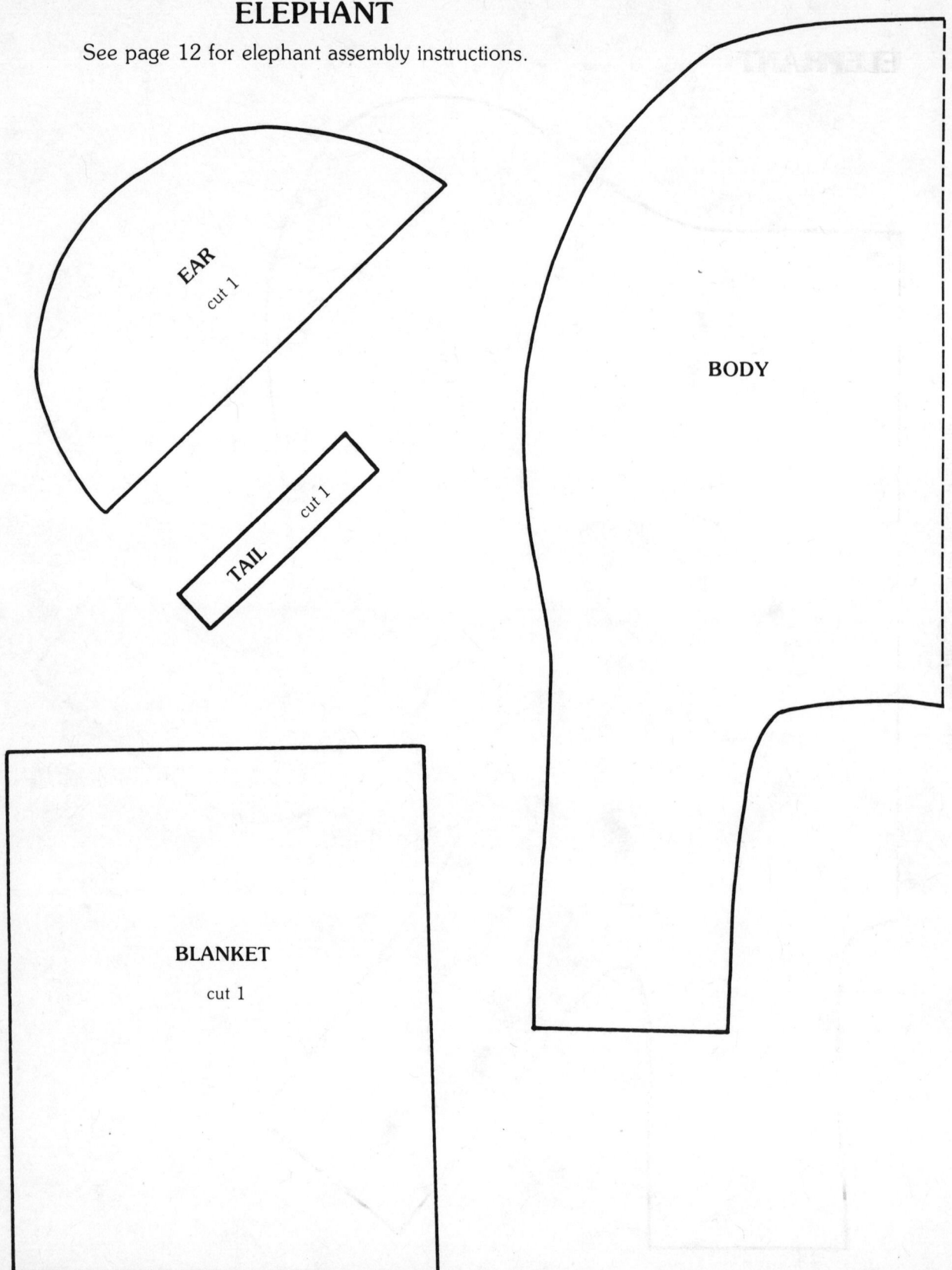

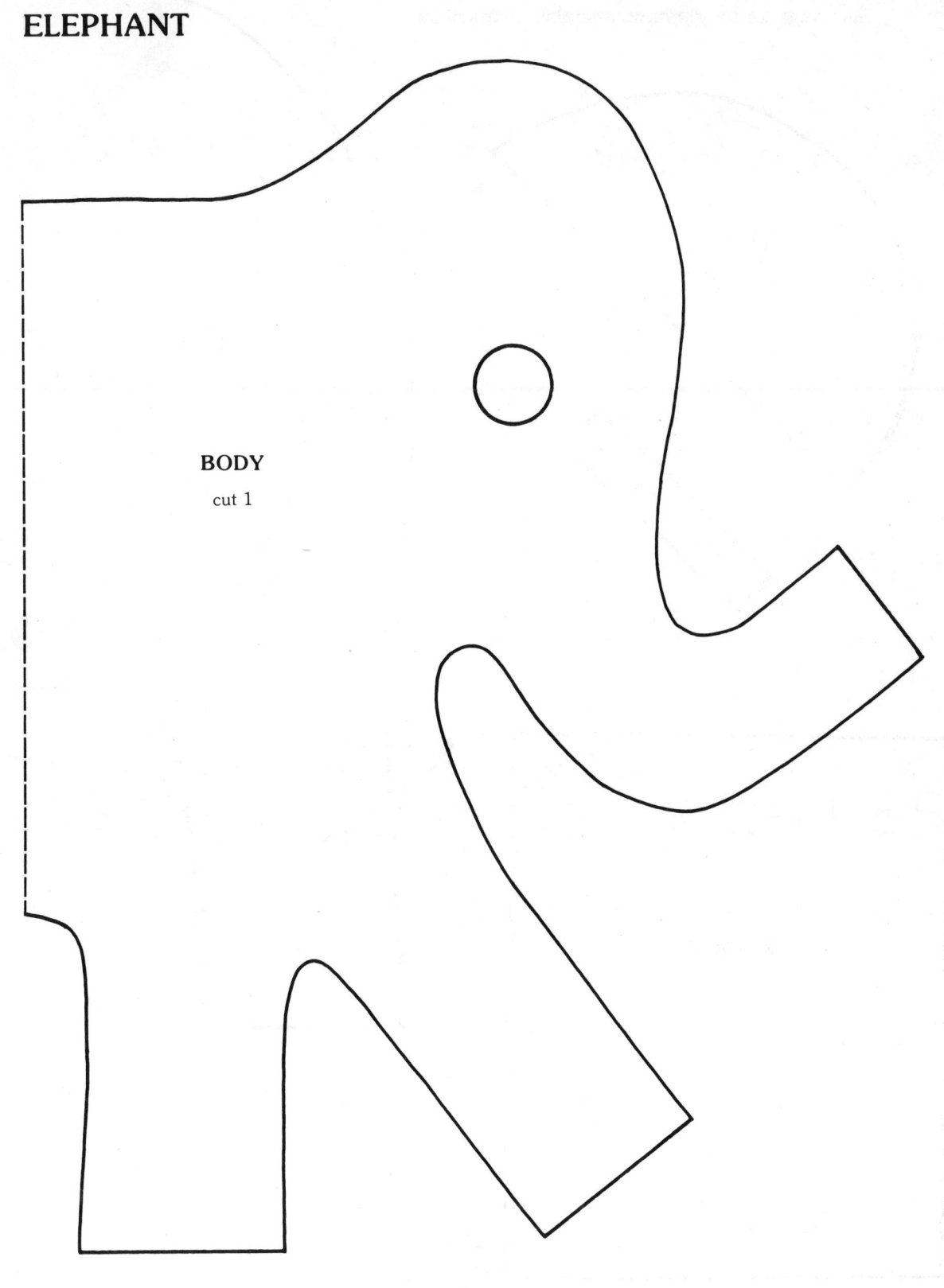

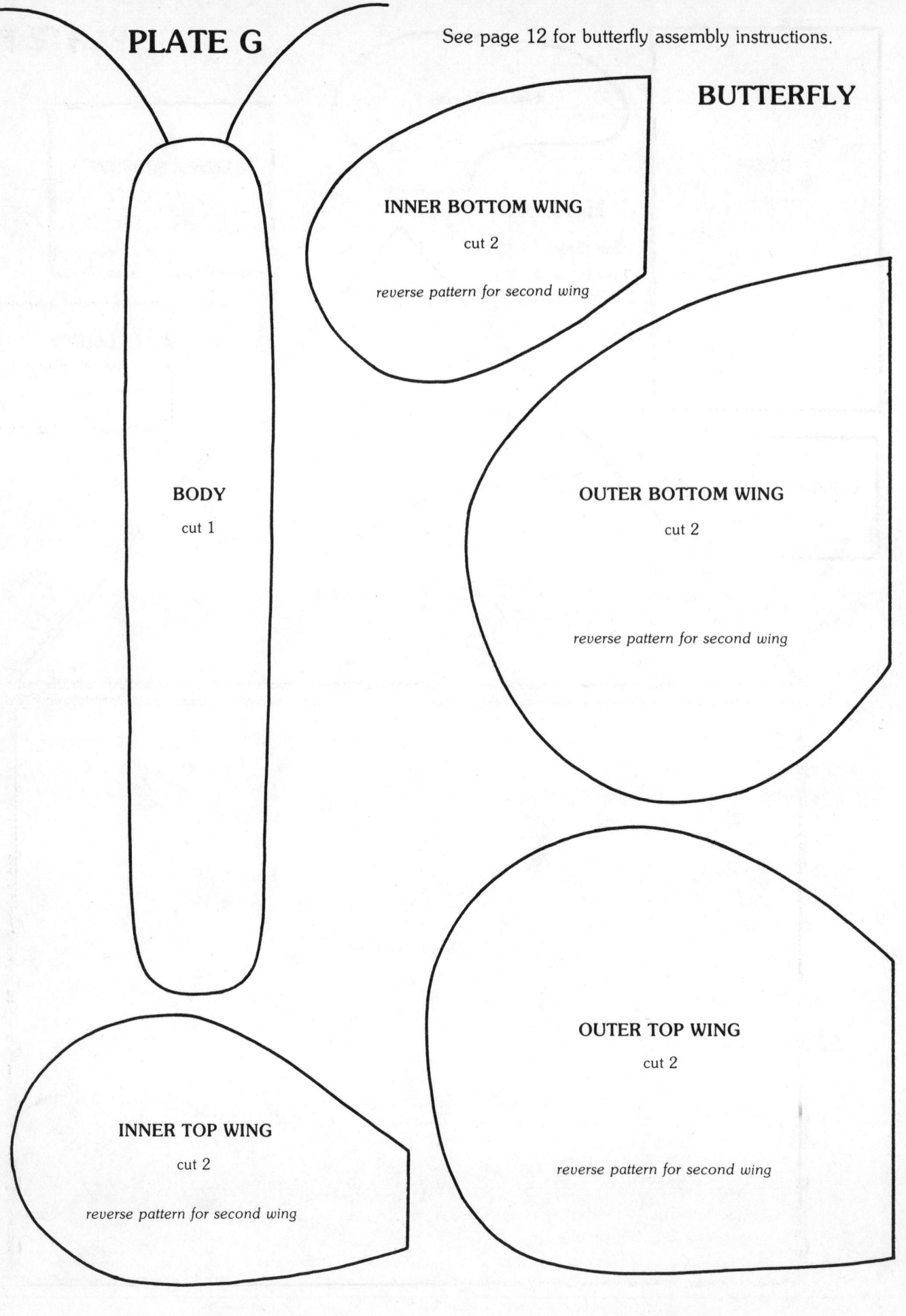

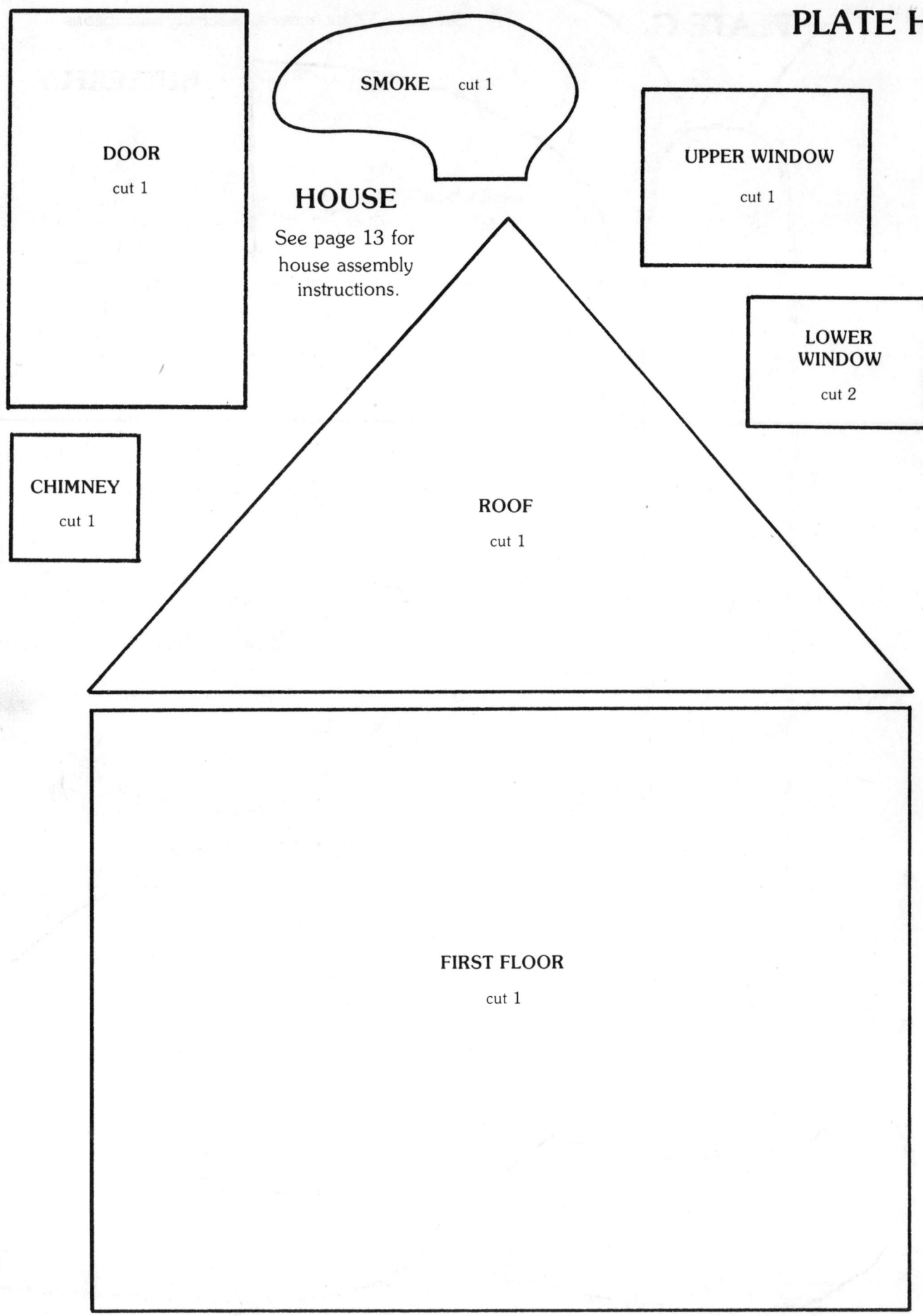

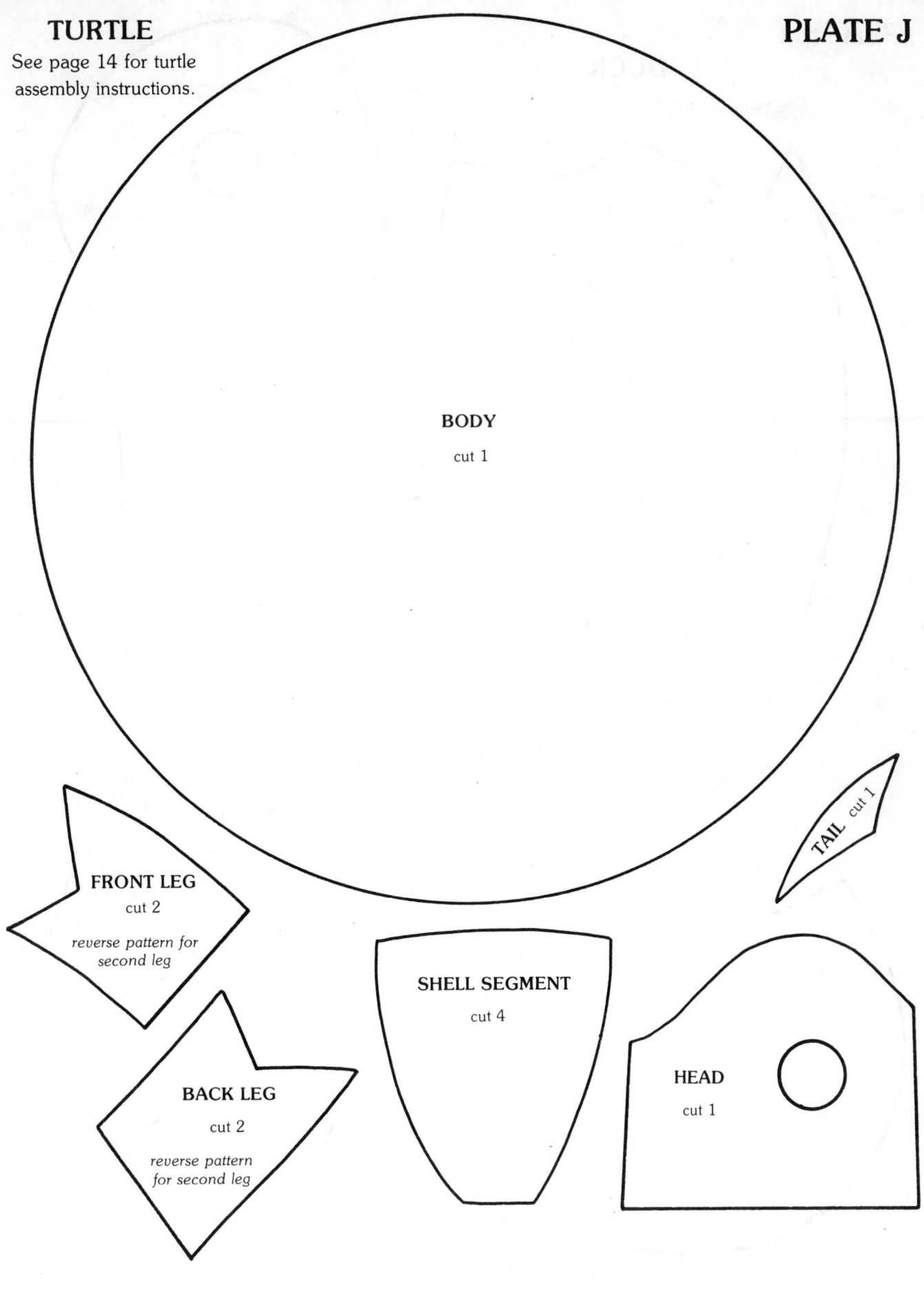

PLATE M

HEART

See page 15 for heart assembly instructions.

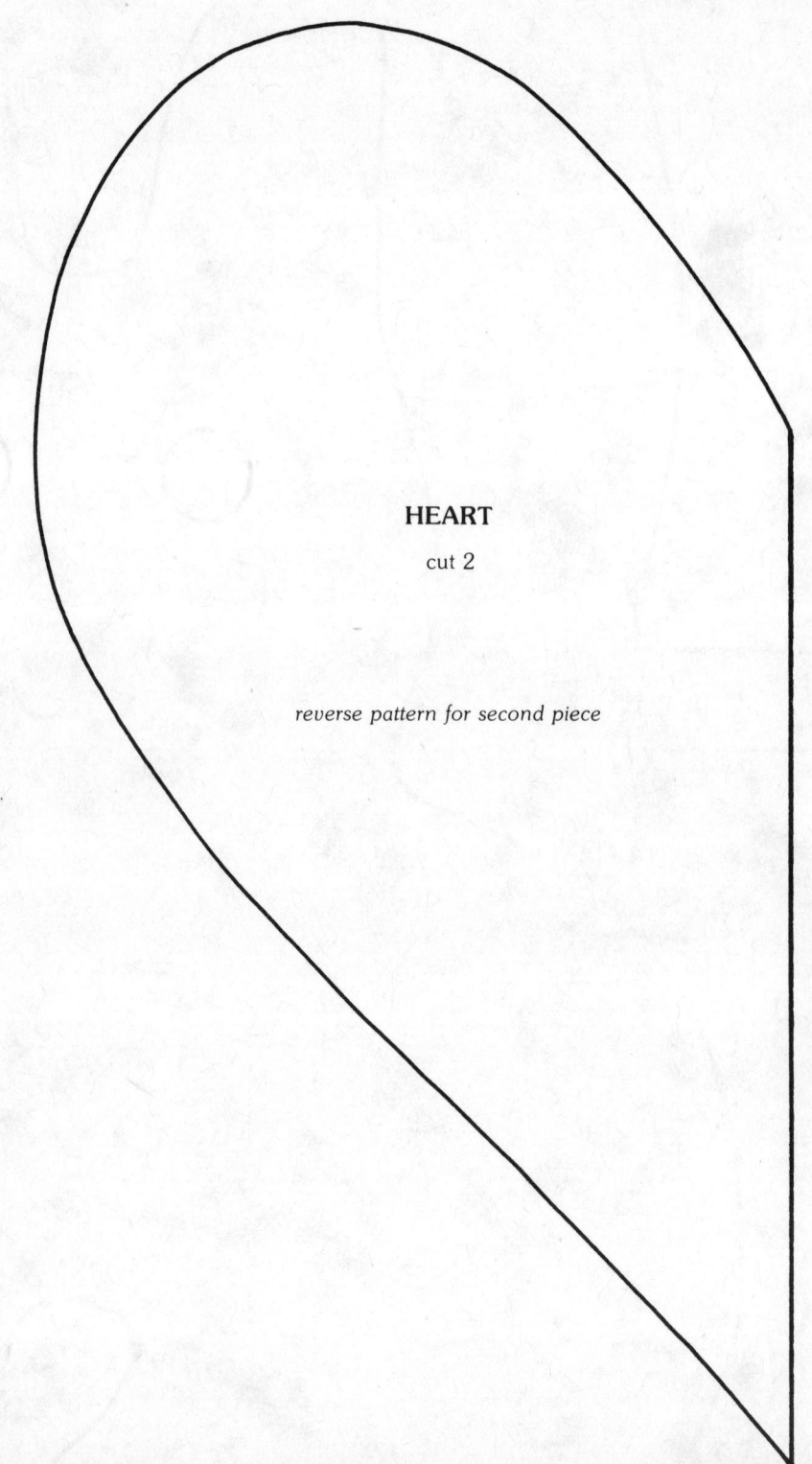

HEART

cut 2

reverse pattern for second piece

PLATE O LADYBUG See page 16 for ladybug assembly instructions.

HEAD
cut 1

SPOT
cut 2

BODY
cut 1

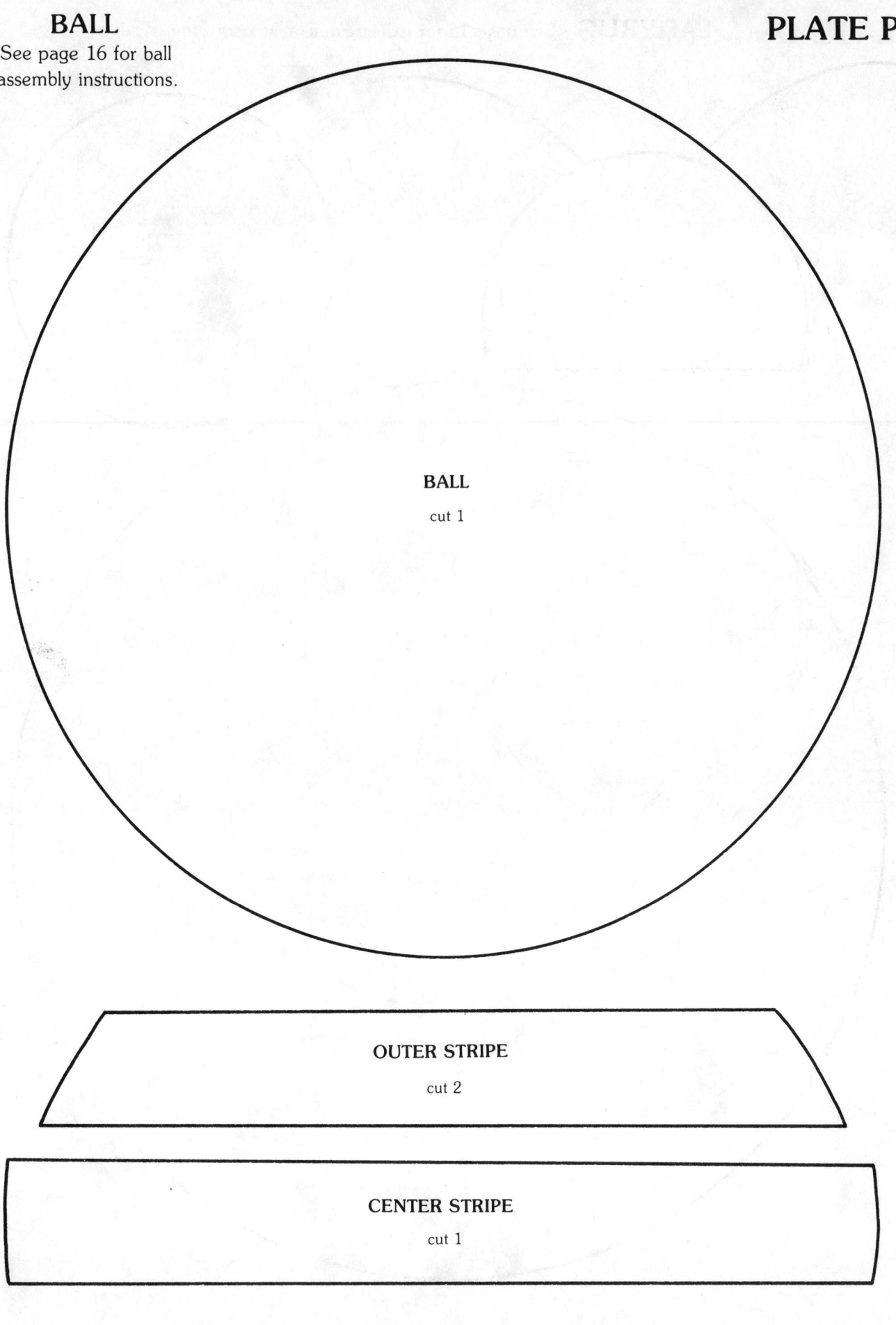

Instructions (continued)

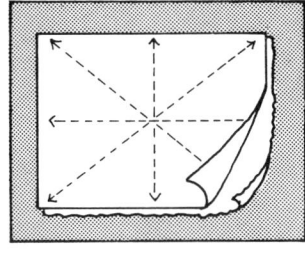

Diagram 10

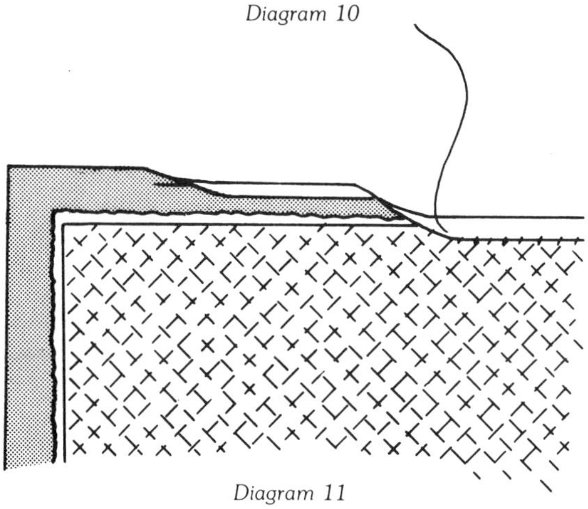

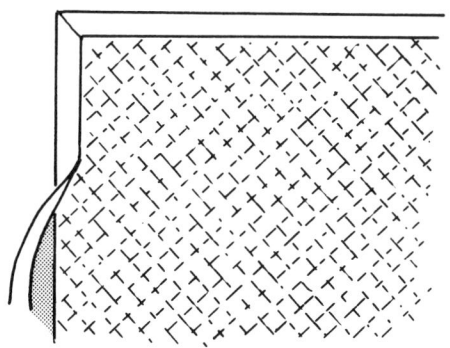

Diagram 11

Diagram 12

raw edge of the lining fabric ½" to the wrong side (which really is the side facing you) and baste in place. Fold the lining fabric over the edge of the quilt top, making a ¾" border all around the quilt (Diagram 11); pin, baste and blind-stitch in place, mitering the corners (Diagram 12).

Tufting

Tufting will secure the three sections of the quilt "sandwich"; you will need a large-eyed needle and embroidery floss or orlon acrylic yarn. Follow Diagram 13. Thread the needle with floss or yarn; starting on the right side or quilt top, draw the floss or yarn through all three layers, then back up to the right side (1). Tie the ends in a double knot (2, 3). Tuft at each corner of each quilt block, then trim all the ends so they are even (about 1" long). Remove any basting stitches that are left on the quilt.

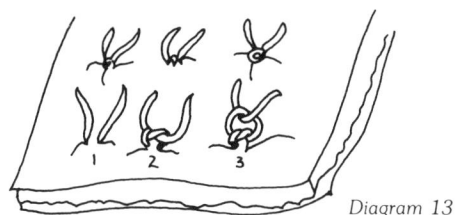

Diagram 13

The Finishing Touch

The last step in making any quilt is to add your signature and the date the quilt was completed. Write your name or initials and the date in pencil on the lower right quilt block. Using a contrasting color embroidery thread, embroider your pencil lines in outline stitch. You can also embroider the name or initials of the child who will be sleeping under the quilt for an extra-special touch.

METRIC CONVERSION CHART

CONVERTING INCHES TO CENTIMETERS AND YARDS TO METERS

mm — millimeters   cm — centimeters   m — meters

INCHES INTO MILLIMETERS AND CENTIMETERS
(Slightly rounded off for convenience)

inches	mm		cm	inches	cm	inches	cm	inches	cm
1/8	3mm			5	12.5	21	53.5	38	96.5
1/4	6mm			5½	14	22	56	39	99
3/8	10mm	or	1cm	6	15	23	58.5	40	101.5
1/2	13mm	or	1.3cm	7	18	24	61	41	104
5/8	15mm	or	1.5cm	8	20.5	25	63.5	42	106.5
3/4	20mm	or	2cm	9	23	26	66	43	109
7/8	22mm	or	2.2cm	10	25.5	27	68.5	44	112
1	25mm	or	2.5cm	11	28	28	71	45	114.5
1¼	32mm	or	3.2cm	12	30.5	29	73.5	46	117
1½	38mm	or	3.8cm	13	33	30	76	47	119.5
1¾	45mm	or	4.5cm	14	35.5	31	79	48	122
2	50mm	or	5cm	15	38	32	81.5	49	124.5
2½	65mm	or	6.5cm	16	40.5	33	84	50	127
3	75mm	or	7.5cm	17	43	34	86.5		
3½	90mm	or	9cm	18	46	35	89		
4	100mm	or	10cm	19	48.5	36	91.5		
4½	115mm	or	11.5cm	20	51	37	94		

YARDS TO METERS
(Slightly rounded off for convenience)

yards	meters	yards	meters	yards	meters	yards	meters	yards	meters
1/8	0.15	2 1/8	1.95	4 1/8	3.80	6 1/8	5.60	8 1/8	7.45
1/4	0.25	2 1/4	2.10	4 1/4	3.90	6 1/4	5.75	8 1/4	7.55
3/8	0.35	2 3/8	2.20	4 3/8	4.00	6 3/8	5.85	8 3/8	7.70
1/2	0.50	2 1/2	2.30	4 1/2	4.15	6 1/2	5.95	8 1/2	7.80
5/8	0.60	2 5/8	2.40	4 5/8	4.25	6 5/8	6.10	8 5/8	7.90
3/4	0.70	2 3/4	2.55	4 3/4	4.35	6 3/4	6.20	8 3/4	8.00
7/8	0.80	2 7/8	2.65	4 7/8	4.50	6 7/8	6.30	8 7/8	8.15
1	0.95	3	2.75	5	4.60	7	6.40	9	8.25
1 1/8	1.05	3 1/8	2.90	5 1/8	4.70	7 1/8	6.55	9 1/8	8.35
1 1/4	1.15	3 1/4	3.00	5 1/4	4.80	7 1/4	6.65	9 1/4	8.50
1 3/8	1.30	3 3/8	3.10	5 3/8	4.95	7 3/8	6.75	9 3/8	8.60
1 1/2	1.40	3 1/2	3.20	5 1/2	5.05	7 1/2	6.90	9 1/2	8.70
1 5/8	1.50	3 5/8	3.35	5 5/8	5.15	7 5/8	7.00	9 5/8	8.80
1 3/4	1.60	3 3/4	3.45	5 3/4	5.30	7 3/4	7.10	9 3/4	8.95
1 7/8	1.75	3 7/8	3.55	5 7/8	5.40	7 7/8	7.20	9 7/8	9.05
2	1.85	4	3.70	6	5.50	8	7.35	10	9.15

AVAILABLE FABRIC WIDTHS

25"	65cm	50"	127cm
27"	70cm	54"/56"	140cm
35"/36"	90cm	58"/60"	150cm
39"	100cm	68"/70"	175cm
44"/45"	115cm	72"	180cm
48"	122cm		

AVAILABLE ZIPPER LENGTHS

4"	10cm	10"	25cm	22"	55cm
5"	12cm	12"	30cm	24"	60cm
6"	15cm	14"	35cm	26"	65cm
7"	18cm	16"	40cm	28"	70cm
8"	20cm	18"	45cm	30"	75cm
9"	22cm	20"	50cm		

Cat

(templates on Plates A and B)

Prepare all pieces as directed for hand or machine appliqué. Center body on background, then position legs so top edges are beneath body piece; baste. Baste stripes, chest, collar and nose to body. Appliqué all pieces with matching thread. Embroider eyes in satin stitch and mouth in outline stitch.

Owl

(templates on Plates C and D)

Prepare all pieces as directed for hand or machine appliqué. Center body on background, then position legs so top edges are beneath body piece; baste. Baste beak and eyes to body; baste pupils in center of eyes; baste wings to body and background. Appliqué all pieces with matching thread.

Elephant

(templates on Plates E and F)

Prepare all pieces as directed for hand or machine appliqué. Center body on background, then position tail at rear so end of tail is beneath body piece; baste. Baste blanket to body, then baste ear to blanket and body. Appliqué all pieces with matching thread. Embroider eye in satin stitch.

Butterfly

(templates on Plate G)

Prepare all pieces as directed for hand or machine appliqué. With straight edges even, center and baste inner top wings to outer top wings, and inner bottom wings to outer bottom wings. Center body on background, then position wings on each side of body so straight edges are beneath body piece; baste. Appliqué all pieces with matching thread. Embroider antennae in outline stitch.

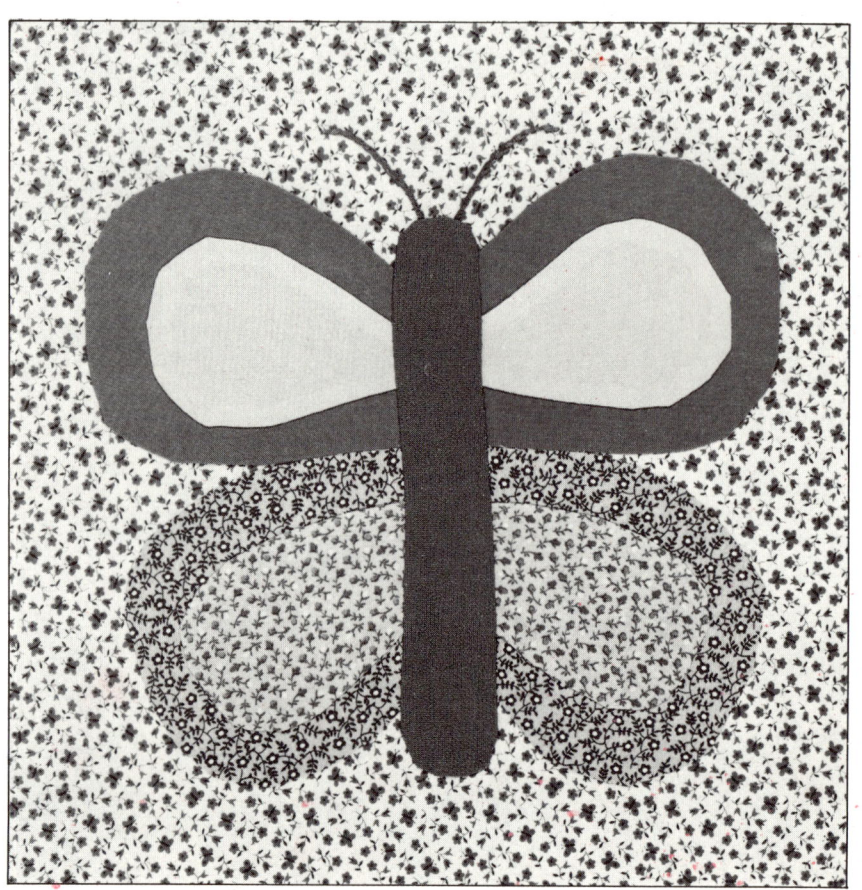

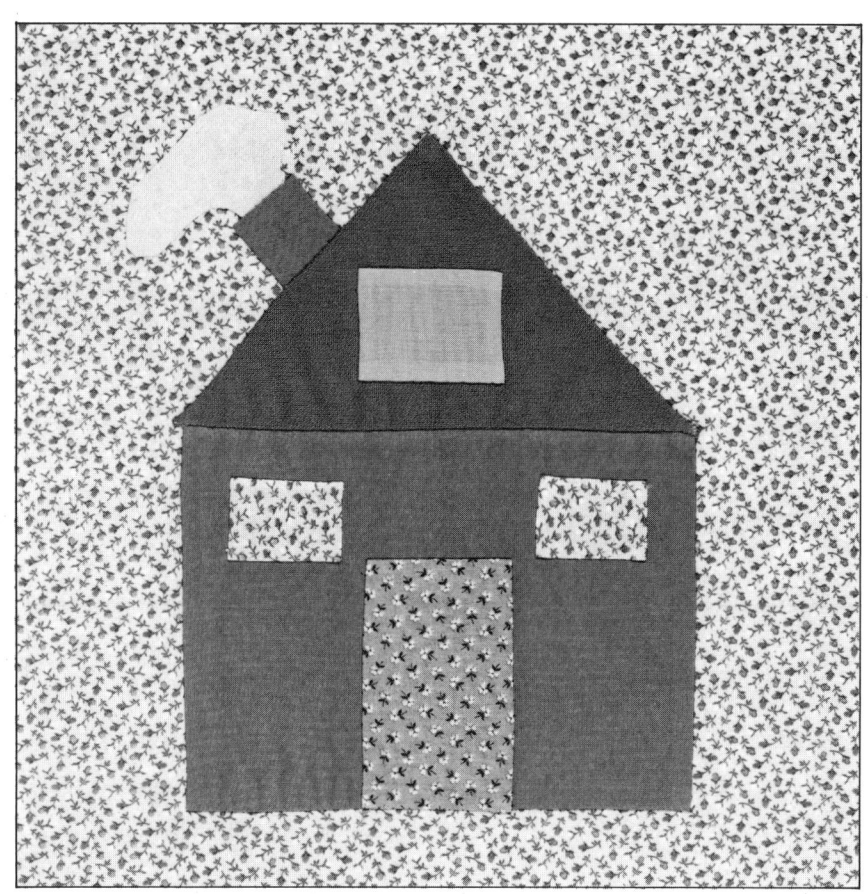

House

(templates on Plate H)

Prepare all pieces as directed for hand or machine appliqué. Center and baste first floor to background. Position roof over first floor, slightly overlapping top edge; baste. Position smoke and chimney on left side of roof, so chimney is flush with roof and slightly overlapping straight edge of smoke; baste. Baste door and windows in place. Appliqué all pieces with matching thread.

Duck

(templates on Plate I)

Prepare all pieces as directed for hand or machine appliqué. Center body on background, then position legs and beak so straight edges are beneath body piece; baste. Baste wing to body. Appliqué all pieces with matching thread. Embroider eye in satin stitch.

Turtle

(templates on Plate J)

Prepare all pieces as directed for hand or machine appliqué. Center body on background, then position legs, head and tail so straight edges are beneath body piece; baste. Baste shell segments, evenly spaced, to body. Appliqué all pieces with matching thread. Embroider eye in satin stitch.

Teddy Bear

(templates on Plates K and L)

Prepare all pieces as directed for hand or machine appliqué. Center and baste body on background. Baste nose and paws to body; baste bow tie to body and background. Appliqué all pieces with matching thread. Embroider eyes and heart in satin stitch and mouth in outline stitch.

Heart

(template on Plate M)

Prepare both pieces as directed for hand or machine appliqué. Position each half of heart on background with straight edges slightly overlapping; baste. Appliqué both pieces with matching thread.

Bunny

(templates on Plate N)

Prepare all pieces as directed for hand or machine appliqué. Center body on background, then position tail at rear so straight edge is beneath body piece; baste. Baste nose to body; baste bow tie to body and background. Appliqué all pieces with matching thread. Embroider eyes in satin stitch and mouth in outline stitch.

Ladybug

(templates on Plate O)

Prepare all pieces as directed for hand or machine appliqué. Center body on background, then position head in place so straight edge is beneath body piece; baste. Baste spots to body. Appliqué all pieces with matching thread. Embroider antennae in outline stitch.

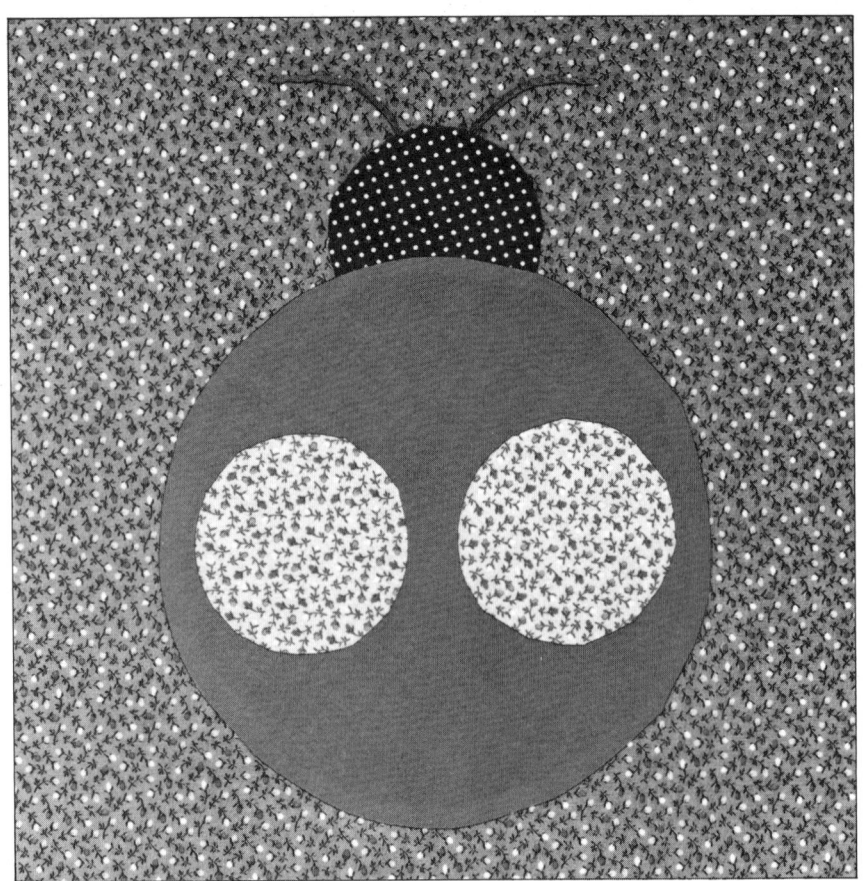

Ball

(templates on Plate P)

Prepare all pieces as directed for hand or machine appliqué. Center ball on background; baste. Baste stripes to ball. Appliqué all pieces with matching thread.